IDOLS AND SINS
CHRISTIANS
LOVE

JIM HOWARD

Lulu Publishing Services rev. date: 02/19/2018

CONTENTS

PREFACE

Author reveals sinful practices, and beliefs of Christians in eye-opening new book. In "Idols and Sins Christians Love," Author answers this question for his readers: What did God really mean when he said, "Thou shalt have no other gods before me?" Not being attentive to God's word, often brings poor foresight and ignorance. God's word reads; "Where there is no vision, the people perish: but he that keepeth the law, happy is he." (Proverbs 29:18 KJV) Being deceived, not knowing it, and not caring, often breeds, "ignorance 'with' apathy;" both of which, 'can and have' lead many to hell.

Author emphasizes that some "modern Christians" worship Satan in ignorance through their practices and idols. The Old and New Testament both talk about "sins of ignorance." For instance, Halloween has always been authored by Satan himself, with Halloween events, parades and parties are flocked with youngsters in witchcraft and satanic costumes. Children look forward to Santa Claus or Saint Nicholas during Christmas, when in fact, Jesus is still the reason for this season. The Easter bunny and his multi-colored eggs hidden everywhere tell a lot about where Christians' hearts are during the Easter season, and what they are teaching their children.

"Idols and Sins Christians Love" reveals the truth to Christian readers on what the Apostle James expressed to his brethren; let's tell the Gentile Christians to abstain from pollutions of idols. (Acts 15:20 KJV) For time and space sake the author deals with just the, "male idol 'Baal' in the 'Old Testament,' in these memoirs," and not the "female Ashtoreth, or the other female goddesses'." In the New Testament, we deal with all idols in and of the heart; however, not all by name.

The Apostle Paul wrote; "For the time will come when they will not endure sound doctrine; but after their own lusts shall they heap to themselves teachers, having itching ears." (2 Timothy 4:3 KJV) According to the scriptures, "Preaching against Idol worship is sound doctrine;" however, our Christian community is filled with idol worship. Just "how sound" is our preaching against idol worship? Paul wrote to Titus; "But speak thou the things 'which become' sound doctrine." (Titus 2:1 KJV) Will "preaching against idolatry" ever become sound doctrine to our Christian community today? If not, "will God 'again' 'wink' at it?" (Acts 17:30 KJV)

The Author reflects the philosophy established in (Psalm 68:11 KJV), "The Lord gave the word, and great was the company of those who published it."

INTRODUCTION

Hi, my name is Jim Howard, and I have been around since the middle of the Great Depression, and I have looked, listened, read, and observed a lot of things, and in some, I have seen a lot of changes. In the things of God, Christians and sinners, and/or believers and unbelievers, both have lost a reality of truth in how holy, jealous, good, angry, and serious our creator is. However, our creator hasn't changed, and on the Day of Judgment, "that will be 'disturbing' too many." (Mal. 3:6; Matt. 7:21–23; KJV).

For you that are reading these memoirs, I pray that you will pray for God's guidance before and after reading them, for they may ruffle your feathers, unless you are really sold out to God. Many in our Christian community don't seem to realize over the years our churches have slowly grown cold and lukewarm, and we are in a precarious place with God. (Revelation 3:16 KJV) Not all, but much of that has to do with, idol worship, and ignorance.

This article originally wasn't written to be a book, but are a collection of "many" memoirs, that I have written over the years. One person read some of my memoirs and mentioned I should put them together in a book. And so I have put "these together", because they concern our Christian communities, which are a combination of denominational churches, "God's elect," and some real nice people that are so holy and good they just don't need God, but they know they are going to heaven. *(Sorry about the long sentence, but let it stay.)* However, don't laugh at that concept, for there are a lot of people like that, who are going to hell, completely unaware; "Except a man be born again, 'he cannot see' the kingdom of God." (John 3:3 KJV)

These see no need in being born again, though they have heard the message often; however, they haven't heard that message, "where their hearts could be pricked by God's two edge sword." Some ministers preach God's word so dry, it's almost powder and chokes and gags would be believers. I have heard some sermons like that myself, and they make me gag. Intentionally, I have been a little bit cynical at times in my putting these memoirs together, for a reason. "I am no Elijah;" however, these scriptures came to me, in 1 Kings 18:27-28 KJV, Elijah got very cynical himself about idol worship.

Other people have mentioned some of this to me, and I have also seen these churches as the development of what Christ said, "Many will say to me in that day, 'Lord, Lord, have we not prophesied in thy name? And in thy name have cast out devils? And in thy name done many wonderful works?' And then will I profess unto them, 'I never knew you: depart from me, ye that work iniquity.'" (Matt. 7:22–23, KJV) That doesn't mean everyone in these churches are lost. But according to Jesus, "many" will be. Remember, Jesus also said; "many" are called "but few" are chosen. (Matt. 22:14, KJV) What does Jesus see in our churches today about the, "many" of what, and "few" of what?

Sometimes I refer to our, "Christian community as knowing Christ"; however, sometimes I refer to them as our, "deceived Christian community, that 'tell people they know Christ'." Bear with me on that. Regardless of these two ways, God has his, "Elect" that are his called, chosen, and faithful. (Revelation 17:14 KJV) Sometimes in my memoirs I write as though, "I am talking to you 'in person'." The reason for that is, "I have talked to 'a lot' of people", who would rather question what I said or write, "instead of listen to what I say or write." I am writing to persons reading these memoirs as, "talking to them, 'or you'." And you will notice, "sometimes 'I ramble a little bit', but bear with me on that as well." Personally, I don't care for rambling preachers. But to get these "memoirs and message" across I intentionally repeat, "somethings."

Remember, Jesus talked about people who would rather question what he said, then listen. Jesus said; "He that hath ears to hear, let him hear." (Matthew 11:15 KJV) I trust that you will listen and hear what I have written from God's word, and understand. Jesus said; "Therefore speak I to them in parables: because they seeing see not; and 'hearing they hear not', neither do they understand."

(Matthew 13:13 KJV) I am trying to write plainly, "and not 'just facts and truth being put' in the back ground."

You will read several short repeated dialogues, which I have had with different people, who didn't care for what I had to write or say in these memoirs. Some of these that I talked to, just wanted to argue. To get these memoirs and message across, I have "intentionally repeated" some scriptures, phrases, and some arguments. I have vaguely used proper words and terms out of place. Some of my grammar and sentence structure are intentionally very graphic, and some are "a little" long, but bear with me on that as well.

These memoirs also reflect a message from Luke (16:19-31 KJV). A Jewish rich man died and went to hell. In his anguish he wanted Abraham to send Lazarus and dip the tip of his finger in water, and cool his tongue; for he was tormented in the flame. Abraham told him that couldn't be, then the rich man was very concerned about his brothers coming there, and ask Abraham to send Lazarus to his brothers that were lost. Somehow this rich man saw his brothers coming to this terrible place called, "Hell." Abraham told him they have Moses and the Prophets to tell them. The rich man wanted Lazarus to be raised from the dead and sent. Abraham said; "if they wouldn't believe Moses and the prophets, they wouldn't believe one coming back from the dead." It has been this way since the begging of man, "When truth is preached, 'many' will not hear or believe it."

This rich man "didn't talk about 'being lost'." He talked

about, "torment in the flame or flames of hell." I'll deal more with this place called, "Hell, and what it is later." How many Christians that are still alive, claim they know God, and his word; yet aren't the least concerned about their loved ones going to hell? Do we have to go to hell to find out how, "real 'hell' is?" Why can't we just, "believe God", and "his word."

What does it take for us to realize, "Hell" isn't going to be a place of comfort, and "those we love" are going there if they are not saved? Many in our Church community have refused the written word of God, and Jesus, "that did 'rise from the dead' and did talk about that place called hell." What does it take sometimes to wake up spiritually dead people, this side of eternity? Think on that, and we know, "The Day of Judgement" is going to wake up, "Many," but then too late.

THE CONGLOMERATE

Many in our 21st Century Christian community and/or our new millennium, cannot see paganism and all its heathenistic ways, "including and mainly the occult," from past generations up to today deeply impregnated into our Christian community. However, it is there in enormous strength. Our churches in general have joined the "conglomerate." What is the conglomerate? I have heard this explained different ways, and this is my short view. The business, social, and world in general, and what Jesus talked about, "Many false prophets from everywhere will deceive many" (My paraphrase of Matt. 24:26 KJV).

One of the biggest structures in this conglomerate is advertising, and news media, manipulated by the antichrist, and further enlarged by people who claim to be the people of God and/or our, "many 'different Christian denominational churches and/or church communities'." Today the Antichrist is alive and well, but will not show his, "Real Evil Face" until (Revelations 13 KJV). However, he does have his many Antichrist's that are doing his work as false prophets and many other things. John called these, "Many Antichrist, 'many deceivers'." (1 John 2:18 - 2 John 1:7 KJV)

This also involves the Illuminati and their/its many cohorts. Our modern day churches love the world, and they are so entangled with the world they cannot see it at all. Satan is the god of this world, and when we love the world, Satan has us even when we are faithful going to church and worshipping God. God has our lips, tongues, and mouths in the church service singing, "Oh how I love Jesus," but Satan has our hearts on the ballgame, hunting, and fishing, and a million other places, where he wants it (2 Cor. 4:4, KJV). We might as well accept the fact, "Satan has people's hearts and souls where he wants them, 'and he is sending them to hell'," but there are, "many of these" that know they are going to heaven. However, Jesus did tell us; "Many were not." (Matthew 7:21 KJV)

CHRISTIAN COMMUNITIES

Again, our new millennium Christian communities are serving and worshipping God, but what God, when there is only one God? Isn't that a crazy question, but maybe not? Satan has convinced "many" to worship him, for he is "god." Down through the millenniums and centuries, Satan has maneuvered many to worship him through idols. After the days of Noah, from the Tower of Babel on, idol worship was slowly penetrating God's creation by man taking it where ever they went, and slowly moving away from Jehovah. In the days of the Kings of Israel, and the prophets, Baal seemed to have a great following, with many forms, names, and pen names. However, Baal is not an idol of the past. It is the biggest idol of our present day, and is presented in many different forms, names, pen names, fraternal societies, "so called 'Christian Communities', and the Islamic idolatry as Allah."

We do have Satan worshippers today. Satan is the god of this world, and many who claim to be Christians are worshipping him by pagan, occult, and heathenistic

practices, "and 'most' of this 'through their ignorance'."
And this is done by deception and maneuvering God's
creation from truth (2 Cor. 4:4, KJV). And so doing, Satan
has made many counterfeits of "God, and of 'Jesus'."
Jesus said, "For many shall come in my name, saying,
'I am Christ'; and shall deceive many" (Matt. 24:5, KJV).
Jesus also said; "Wherefore if they shall say unto you,
Behold, he is in the desert; go not forth: behold, he is in
the secret chambers; believe it not" (Matt. 24:26 KJV).

"Satan counterfeits the 'Real Jesus, the real prophets,
and everything about them', and counterfeits 'works
of wonder'." That false prophet may well be, the best
preacher and pastor in town. If you would yank his sheep
skin off, you would have a, "full grown 'predatory vicious
wolf'," of which he is.

"Oh no, 'not my pastor, he has his doctorate'."

Satan's false prophets don't mind having PHDs. In fact
PHDs are to their advantage.

How many have heard said, "God is really in the
equal rights agenda, because homosexuals were born
that way?" Yes, I have heard Christians entertain that
concept. The "counterfeit god, Christ, and his gospel,
and all of their false prophets, 'Okays the equal rights
agenda';" however, the "Only God", and he is "the 'Holy'
God" doesn't. The God of the Book of Genesis didn't okay
the gay lifestyle then, and he is still the same God, and he
has not changed, according to Mal. 3:6, KJV. Whether we
see it or not, "God's word 'now', including his 'final words
then', will be carried out on 'His' Judgement Day, without

4

any changes of who he is, and what he will do," according to, (Isaiah 55:11 KJV) (Revelations 21:8 KJV).

Again, what Christ are we serving when there is only one? There is only one Christ but "many 'counterfeit Christ or Antichrist'." These counterfeit Christ will come in all shapes and sizes. False prophets preach a counterfeit Christ. Back in Old Testament times, Baal was a counterfeit of Jehovah, but as "evil 'as evil' can get, because Baal was the Devil himself." Any worship status to, "other than God" is worshipping Satan, "in some 'deceptive name' form." Our Christian communities of today would just as soon ignore this prophecy of Jesus in (Matt. 24:5, KJV). If you want to go to heaven, you won't ignore it. How many people, who claim to be Christians, are serving a pagan, occult, heathenistic, counterfeit Christ? According to Jesus, "many" are (Matt. 24:5 KJV).

"Oh surely not Jim! 'That's just your opinion of what Jesus said'!"

"In the beginning was the Word, and the Word was with God, and the Word was God", and that is "My opinion", and it is also, "God's opinion" (John 1:1, KJV). God, his name, his word, and his truth, just doesn't matter anymore to "many" in God's creation. It has been that way from time to time, ever since Lucifer said in his heart, "I will ascend into heaven and put my throne next to the throne of God in heaven, I will exalt my throne above the stars of God: I will sit also upon the mount of the congregation, in the sides of the north." And then Lucifer smeared his lies through the Serpent in the Garden of Eden. It was the

Serpent, Satan, and man that disregarded the truth, not God. God said, "For I am the Lord, I change not" (Mal. 3:6, KJV). Hebrews 13:8 (KJV) tells us; "Jesus Christ the same yesterday, and today, and forever."

John 17:17 (KJV) tells us, "God's word is 'truth'." (Ps. 46:10 KJV) tells us; "Be still, and know that I am God: I will be exalted among the heathen, I will be exalted in the earth." How well do we realize that, or do we even realize it at all? However, before that let's remember, the Lord spoke to Adam and Eve, saying, "Of every tree in the garden you may eat freely: But the tree of knowledge of good and evil, you shall not eat: for in the day you eat it you shalt surely die" (Gen. 2:16–17, KJV).

What God said was truth! The truth meant little to Eve, when she, in "her 'whim'," thought she would be like God. That "momentary whim" was a beautiful insight for an action, and everything would be better than what I have now, "and oh what deception, 'I'll be like God'." All of that was and is the seed and work of deception. For the moment, this is the thing to believe and do. This covers just about every avenue of our heart, mind, and soul, and that is a big target for deception that brings about a lot of detouring our hearts and souls from truth.

How often do we evade the truth when we want or see something that makes us more attractive to all, as well as ourselves for the moment? Satan is skilled in deception to alter what man knows as truth, and boy does mankind fall for it, hook, line, and sinker. The equal rights people use the views of, "equal rights" to evade and pervert

God's truth, and so many are deceived and don't see that. Lucifer set the stage for that deception, "I'll be like God." But he wasn't like God! Then; "Eve, 'you will be like God', but she wasn't like God." This also includes people "who claim" to be Christians today, "but aren't." Only the elect are not deceived; however, when God thinks his elect could or might be deceived, He removes them, or will have his angels remove them at the right time (Matt. 24:22 - Mark 13:20, KJV).

God said, "Therefore shall a man leave his father and his mother, and shall cleave unto his wife: and they shall be one flesh" (Gen. 2:24, KJV). This was truth. In Noah's day, people could not handle Noah preaching righteousness and/or truth, and they chose to ignore the truth. They chose to have as many wives as they wanted. However, God dwelt severely with their wickedness. And God saw that the wickedness of man was great in the earth, and that every imagination of the thoughts of his heart was only evil continually (Gen. 6:5, KJV). Has the heart of man ever changed any? According to Jesus, it hasn't (Mark 7:21 KJV). However, "maybe" our hearts have gotten worse, if that is possible?

Today, look at our youth, and some are just kids, way too young to get married and be one flesh. Yet they run around like wild animals or stray dogs, with no proper teaching, young kids having sex with anyone that's handy, having babies born and raised out of wedlock without any kind of parental protocol. Children having children, and neither have a mom or dad, and we are equal rights civilized people. Sex has become a god or idol of the heart to many; however, if not an idol, let's make it an idol, and "many 'on the left' will." I wish not; however "many" in our Christian community will also.

Our "Equal Rights Agenda", which controls our main line media, have been viciously teaching young kids have "rights" to not be "forced to be taught decency!" Young kids have a right to experiment with any and all of their sexual curiosities, straight or gay. The equal rights crowd's attitude is, "only bigots disapprove" of all kinds of sexual pleasure, lewdness, and plenty of all of that.

Handing out condoms at school, instead of truth and proper education, is politically correct. How much more wicked and mindless can our USA get? We are producing swarms of human beings as strays or orphans, much like we let dogs in our neighborhoods produce puppies without any dog owner's control. Some do send the loose/ stray puppies to the dog pounds. A dog pound isn't the best place to send a stray dog; however, it is better than no place.

A lot of our "out of wedlock born" babies are nothing but strays, unless someone adopts them, and if not, we send them to the pound, where we send other baby human orphan strays. However, we don't call it a pound, but maybe we should. We call it/them foster homes. Foster parents are better than no parents, and what I have seen and witnessed, they are usually better than the real biological mom and/or dad, who were and are nothing but loose strays themselves.

Recently I heard on the news some foster homes aren't the best place for some strays. Some self-centered couples are adopting, and/or taking into their homes being foster parents, to use their fostered kids for their added financial pleasure. I didn't like writing that either, but you know it is the truth. Read the newspapers and listen to the radio and TV news, and you will hear about what I just wrote, because that is where I read, heard, and saw it.

I have met some of these young strays, and some go to church, claim to believe in God, and some claim to be Christians. Our Christian communities today are full of all kinds of young human stray beings. We have young stray kids, seemingly without a mom or dad, in our churches. Where is God's Word and/or truth in the hearts of youngster strays that live like this? These strays need Jesus; however, they do not get Jesus in the Christian community that Okays their sins, because that Christian community doesn't know Jesus themselves. According to Jesus, many working for God, "just don't know God," and on the Day of Judgment, God/Jesus won't know them (Luke 13:27; Matt. 7:23 KJV). We could say it this way, and it is the truth; "Our churches are full of religious strays, knowing they are going to heaven, when they are going to hell."

"Oh, 'surely not', not all of them?"

What happened to "Train up a child in the way he should go: and when he is old, he will not depart from it?" (Prov. 22:6, KJV) Is that Scripture just a passing fancy? "Many" have learned there are a lot of scriptures that are no longer up-to-date, because they trespass on our entertainment and sexual pleasure. We are saved by grace now, and those, "Yesterday Bible Teachings" don't apply now. We better get back to believing, and accept the fact; "God's word hasn't changed, won't change, or get 'out of date', and those "Yesterday Bible Teachings," are the only teachings that will get us to heaven. Being "saved by Grace", hasn't changed God's word or message against sin and repentance.

A while back I visited with a young single mom that claimed she was a "Born Again Child of God." I read her a scripture about what Jesus said about fornication. She said, "I have been in church all my life and never heard that." Many of our Christian communities are social fraternal clubs. Some are nothing but enemies of the gospel of Christ, and/or enemies of the cross. Preaching truth, and especially against sin, is biblically, religiously, socially, and politically incorrect, because it detours our sexual gratifications, "which are natural." When our Christian communities are as ungodly as the world, why even claim to be a Christian? The world does not reject anyone for this wickedness; however, on the Day of Judgment, Jesus will. Let me word this another way, Jesus said; "No Church members aloud in heaven, 'just Christians'." However, many "who 'call themselves Christians', don't know the difference."

HALLOWEEN

The following is one abominable worships that our Christian community commits without any spiritual convictions, and they know they are going to heaven. I have "dear 'Christian' friends" that participate in this, and they know they are right with God. How could this be a sin of ignorance? I am aware not all Christians are guilty of this deception, in how people worship Satan, "but they 'are few'." Not all church groups associate with these "occult practices," but I have witnessed many do. Before God convicted me, and dwelt with me about them, "being deceived, 'I was one of them'."

Here is a place where many are directly worshiping the devil, though they deny it, because they are deceived, "and/or 'unenlightened'" on what they are doing. They don't call it a birthday party, but "some of our Christian community churches" give Satan "the 'biggest birthday party' you can imagine every year." Oh, how we and our children have fun at his birthday parties. I know devout Christians that go on and on how their children love the

Halloween season, with all its pleasures, including all the tricks and treats, with their kids dressed up like goblins, witches, and devils.

These know they are going to heaven; however, if "they are" doing this in ignorance, God "may" wink at it. But that whole scenario is dangerous, and it scares the day light out of me. You have to be really ignorant, "to gamble with your soul." The Apostle Paul wrote in (Acts 17:28-30 KJV); "For in him we live, and move, and have our being; as certain also of your own poets have said, for we are also his offspring. Forasmuch then as we are the offspring of God, we ought not to think that the Godhead is like unto gold, or silver, or stone, graven by art and man's device. And the times of this ignorance God winked at; but now commandeth all men everywhere to repent:"

I personally grew up in a church that had Halloween parties for the youth. I went to them and had the time of my life, among other things. It took me years, to learn what I was doing was one of the occult practices. I did some praying and repenting over that. "I did it in ignorance" and "deception." All through that I didn't question my position in Christ. However, when I discovered the truth of what I was doing, "God 'dwelt' with me 'seriously'."

Again, I don't really know this other than what I read in the scriptures; however, "how much 'ignorance'," does God have to put up, "With 'His' people" today, "not knowing 'His' ways today?" Why aren't pastors teaching against the occult and idol worship? Maybe they just don't know any better, and have that, "ignorance status themselves." Didn't they learn anything in College and Seminary? Sometimes when we "don't see 'a lot of wrong' in something, we just accept it" as "nothing, to be concerned about." Just a little bit, "of 'impurity' may not hurt you, and you may not even feel it;" however, the continuation, "may kill you, and send you to the, 'grave yard, and then' hell."

I do believe God is often longsuffering with his people, "waking up and repenting." Again, remember God was longsuffering with Noah's day people, and they repented not and were lost in the flood (1 Pet. 3:20, KJV). God's true people, when they/we hear the truth, will repent. However, today, our Christian community is so spiritually dumbed down and/or backslidden they don't even see what they are doing at times, and many will go to hell over that, because they see "Satan" in his "Halloween season sanctuary" as "that angel of light", with all its worldly glory and "innocent pleasures." *(Sorry about that long sentence.)* The Apostle John wrote; "Love not the world, neither the things that are in the world. If any man love the world, the love of the Father 'is not' in him" (1 John 2:15, KJV).

"Oh, 'surely not', anyway what is wrong with, 'just the fun' in Halloween?"

"That 'just the fun' in Halloween 'is worshiping Satan', and you not believing 'it' doesn't change 'it'." We as Christians, "must become 'Bible students'." Jesus said; "Search the scriptures; for in them 'ye think' ye have eternal life: and they are they which testify of me," (John 5:39). One of the things that this, "Jesus would teach us from the scriptures, of which he is, 'Many false prophets would come and deceive many'." We don't know all the ways these false prophets will plant deception, but most of it will sound like gospel truth, "reasoned and taught" by a false prophet, who may be, "known 'as the best pastor' in town."

When will people, "who call themselves Christians" see that they have endorsed the occult, we have indorsed Baal-worship, and have indorsed Satan himself? We, in our Christian community, don't dress up our children and send them to Sunday school and church to worship God near like we dress up our children like ghosts, goblins, and spooks of all kinds to celebrate the occult big time. Do we love Satan more than we love God? "It appears we do." I am not writing about the world doing these things. Again, I am writing about people who call themselves the people of God and/or Christians. Judgment must begin at the house of God, but when are we going to let it? (1 Pet. 4:17, KJV)

I have gone to church and have seen young ladies singing in the choir wearing short shorts, and I have heard people comment about it, that it shouldn't be, but it continued. They covered up their bodies more than that when they were out tricks and treating. In Genesis the third chapter, God didn't like the bikini style clothes Adam and Eve made out of fig leaves to cover up their nakedness, so he made them coats of animal skins. Why can't Christians at least read and study the first three chapters in the Holy Bible, for God prepared a lot better dress code, than our modern worldly, and our Christian community's dress codes of today.

I have been told; "Jim, you have visited the wrong churches."

"Maybe I have."

Some of our Christian community spend more time in spook houses than in church houses. We even go to the big discount stores and buy things for our children that will make them stand out with spooky reflections to honor Satan, not knowing what we are doing, "but oh how 'Satan' is blessed." Not everyone in our, "Christian Community Churches 'are spiritually minded', but don't you dare 'tell them that'." I tried that, and "I got 'straighten out', on being 'too legalistic'."

This is part of the conglomerate and/or illuminati set up over the past millenniums by Satan for many to follow. "And many" not seeing that it is one of the "Broadways" that leads to destruction. "These many" know they are Christians going to heaven (Matt. 7:13, KJV), but they are not, "unless" they get saved.

Why don't we go to the big discount stores and buy our children clothes that will make them look more like a Christian than a spook. At least buy them clothes that look decent when they go to church, school, and play! I know I have gone to meddling again, but how are we going to meddle our way out of Jesus saying, "Depart from me you worker of iniquity," on the Day of Judgment? The answer is, "we won't." If you are a lover of this world, "and 'its god, which is Satan,' don't count on going to heaven." Your worship in the Occult/Halloween season, "tells God and us 'who you are, and love'." You saying, "God looks on the heart, not the outward appearance", won't work here either. God is looking for hearts that are perfect toward him, not hearts that are full of the world. (2 Chronicles 16:9 KJV) People whose hearts are perfect toward God, don't run-around, "indecently dressed, and/or looking like spooks in that yearly Halloween season."

"But, 'won't Jesus see we were deceived and ignorant, and look over it'?"

Again read, "Matthew 24:11 and Acts 17:30 KJV." When "you have read and/or heard the truth", don't count on, "God 'winking at your ignorance' and let you into heaven."

"But God has to give us time to get straightened out."

"It doesn't take six month to repent and believe the gospel;" however, it may take six months, "or much longer" to learn the scriptures, and to grow in grace, abound in grace, and be taught by grace, and in the things of God, by staying in church. Today is the day of decision/ salvation, "not tomorrow, or six months from now, for Jesus may come tonight, 'or earlier'." My paraphrase of (2 Corinthians 6:2 KJV).

Don't worry, I am going to do some more meddling. I am aware of Christians that hate the Halloween season because of the occult celebrations, and I am one of them. I don't like "One Nation Under God" paying tribute to the occult big time. What Christians should do on Halloween is for churches to be packed with people resisting the devil, praising and worshiping God, "from the depth of 'their hearts, mouths, and tongues, and that all together at the same time' in one place, but when will that happen?"

Oh, how we love to worship Satan, and Satan wants that worship. Again, back in the beginning, Lucifer/Satan tried to put his throne close to God's for his own self-indulgence, but that didn't work. It appears here Lucifer may have tried to set his throne above Gods; "For thou hast said in thine heart, I will ascend into heaven, I will exalt my throne 'above the stars of God: I will sit also upon the mount of the congregation, in the sides of the north'," (Isaiah 14:13 KJV). Lucifer was kicked out of heaven over that scheme. Jesus said; "I beheld Satan as lightning fall from heaven." (Luke 10:18 KJV)

Satan couldn't get Jesus in the wilderness to fall down and worship him, but boy how he has deceived people who claim to be Christ's children to worship him. We do not see that at all because we are so spiritually dumbed down, deceived, and the product of being a, "religious 'Christian' heathen." There may not be such a "thing or thang" as a, "religious 'Christian' heathens", but there is now, because "that is what 'many' in our 'present Christian community are'."

"Jim, you are jumping at conclusions, 'again'."

No I am not, because "many 'on Halloween' treat Satan like he is Christ himself," and they are faithful to worship him that way. Jesus said, "Many shall come in my name, saying, I am Christ; and shall deceive many" (Matt. 24:5, KJV). If we love our Lord God Jehovah so much, why do we give Satan such a great big Halloween party and praise him with so much fun with all our extremely decorated decorum? Oh, how Satan has deceived us into believing; "Halloween is just a great innocent fun time for children, and many Christians believe that." However, Halloween is such an innocent time of fun, in sending souls to, "That 'Devil's Hell'."

"Oh surely not, when we 'really love Jesus'!"

Again, "oh surely yes." You can't love Satan and God both at the same time. It's time for "many" to stop saying, "Oh surely not", and start saying, "Amen." Anyway, if we love Jesus so much, why do we Christians give, "Satan such a 'great big Halloween party'?" We need to mess up his parties, by resisting him, not add to him. The Apostle James wrote; "Submit yourselves therefore to God, 'resist the devil', and he will flee from you." (James 4:7 KJV) It's hard to resist the Devil when you love him so, "and 'dressed up' looking like him on Halloween." Just think on that!

I am aware that many sincere Christians are not even aware of what Halloween is, and being naive is very dangerous; however, I believe God sees their heart is perfect toward him, "that is 'if it is'?" (2 Chron. 16:9 KJV) However, how many of these will wake up on that Great Judgment Day and find out Jesus doesn't know them at all?

Jim, "surely 'sincere Christians' won't have that problem at all?"

Again, are these that claim to be Christians and are doing all of these things and worshipping Satan "really sincere Christians," or just good church members? Being a good church member, gives you no statuesque on Judgment Day. No true Christian is going to hell; however, "many 'good/true church members' will." There can be a lot of difference between, "real good 'church' members," and "real good 'Christians'."

"Oh surely not? 'Most church members are Christians'."

"You tell that to Jesus on the Day of Judgment."

"Jesus already knows that."

"Jesus may have a 'different opinion' than you."

Jim, "Jesus may have a different opinion than you also."

I have already learned that; however. Jesus and I both have agreed on this; "Satan is the god of this world," and "Halloween is one of his 'amusement park segments, sanctuaries, and playgrounds'." In 2 Corinthians 4:4 (KJV), The Apostle Paul wrote; "In whom the god of this world hath blinded the minds of them which believe not, lest the light of the glorious gospel of Christ, who is the image of God, should shine unto them." God said, "You shall have 'no other gods' before me." (Exodus 20:3) People knowing they are Christians, showing up on the Day of Judgment with other gods in the pockets, hearts, and lives, are going to have big problem convincing God, "I don't really love and worship these other things, 'I do them just for fun'."

There are people who commit adultery, "just for fun." Some do it, "just for money."

You may kid yourself now; however, I have a feeling you won't kid Judge Jesus on "His" Judgment Day. Loving

Halloween, "is an idol and/or god, and that idol is of the heart and in the heart, and you do not want to have it in your pocket, or any place else, on Judgment Day." And today is "that day" to get rid of it. Read 2 Corinthians 6:2 (KJV) again. Often, "It's 'not' an 'Easy Road' we are traveling to heaven, but following Jesus, "it is a, 'Holy Road', through a 'strait gate' and 'narrow way'."

Here is what Jesus said; "My sheep 'hear my voice', and 'I know them', and 'they follow me:' and 'I give unto them eternal life'; and 'they shall never perish', neither shall any man pluck them out of my hand." (John 10:27-28 KJV) You may claim to be a Christian; however, if you "haven't heard the voice of Jesus", and "he doesn't know you," and "you aren't following him", don't claim to have eternal life, because you don't. Don't say you do, "and call Jesus 'a liar'."

Israel worshipping Baal in the days of Elijah isn't any more sinful than enjoying "occult pleasures" on Halloween. In fact, paying tribute to Satan on Halloween, "is 'Pure Baal worship', of the Old Testament, though we give it a different name." We could call it, "Baal-spook."

When Israel wondered at the desolation that was coming to them, God's word reads, "Because they have forsaken the covenant of the Lord their God, and worshipped other gods, and served them." (Jer. 22:9 KJV) When will our Christian communities see and understand the occult and God don't mix and never will? We can't serve both! But "many" will keep trying, being deceived, and then go to hell. You don't have to be one of them.

The elect of God gives absolutely no tribute to the occult; however, our so-called Christian communities gives a lot of tribute there, because that is a big part of their deception structured by false prophets, and/or "phony 'not caring' pastors." Our Christian communities that are okaying all the pleasure of Halloween are sending many souls to hell; however, you don't dare tell them that, or you will be criticized like the prophet Elijah "for 'just' troubling" our Christian community. (1 Kings 18:17 KJV) God, help us to wake up! Again, only the truth in God's word will wake us up; however, that won't wake us up if we don't read or hear it, then believe it, "and then be 'a doer' of the word," (James 1:22 KJV).

If Joshua were here today, this is "my rewording" of what he would ask: "If it seems evil to you to serve the Lord, choose you this day whom ye will serve; whether the god of Halloween/world, or the God of Heaven; but as for me and my house, we will serve the God of Heaven," (Josh. 24:15 KJV). Again Jesus said, "Strait is the gate, and narrow is the way, which leadeth unto life, and 'few' there be that find it," (Matt. 7:14 KJV). Halloween is the opposite direction from, "That Strait Gate and Narrow Way, and Satan's false prophets leads 'no one' to it."

According to Jesus in John 17:11 (KJV), his disciples were "in the world;" however, in John 15:19 and John 17:14 (KJV), Jesus said, his disciples were not "of the world." Not of the world, and in the world, are two different things. When you have entered that strait gate and narrow way, you have found Jesus Christ and are still in this world, but no longer of this world, and because of that, Jesus said; "the world would 'hate you'," (John 15:19 KJV). When you accepted Christ as your personal savior, the occult and all of, "its glory" in and "of the world", has to go. Again, 1st John 2:15 (KJV) reads: "Love not the world, neither the things that are in the world. If any man love the world, the love of the Father is not in him."

True Christians that are God's elect and Halloween don't mix and/or entertain each other; however, I have known some of God's people border on deception. Of course I didn't know all the circumstances or see their heart like God does. I did wonder if God is dealing with them. I do pray for them. Jesus did say, "As many as I love, I rebuke and chasten: be zealous therefore, and repent" (Rev. 3:19, KJV). Why would Jesus rebuke those he loves? Because "he loves" them, "even when they sin." But remember he also told them, "be zealous and repent." Again, I have been there, done that, and sometimes it's trying. I think we always need to think and pray about, "Christians 'bordering on deception'." That is a serious anxiety.

Wherefore the Lord said, "Forasmuch as this people draw near me with their mouth, and with their lips do honour me, but have removed their heart far from me, and 'their fear toward me is taught by the precept of men'." In Matthew 15:7-9 (KJV) Jesus also said; "But in vain they do worship me, teaching for doctrines the commandments of men." If your pastor is, "Teaching and Okaying interacting with the Occult", he is a false prophet, "for that 'is not' the doctrine of Christ." However, he could be just an, "ignorant pastor."

"But how will we ever enjoy, living for God, so straight laced?"

Many have found serving God; "Is joy unspeakable and 'full of glory'."

Many of God's people, are not even aware there is an intense war going on between God and Satan. Some Christians don't see we have a "political, spiritual, 'civil war' going on in our USA." Back two thousand years ago, the Apostle Paul wrote; "For we wrestle not against flesh and blood, but against principalities, against powers, against the rulers of the darkness of this world, against spiritual wickedness in high places." There has never been a time that scripture has been more up to date than now. That war is, "This 'War' now." (Ephesians 6:12 KJV) This war won't be over until the Great White Throne Judgement, when God settles all scores. (Revelations 21:8 KJV)

Much of that war in our churches "now," are between "so called saints", against "real saints", and sometimes it is hard to tell, "Which" is "which." We could write or say it this way; "The war is between the 'saved and deceived', but that would upset some people who are, 'a little' deceived, and maybe 'a lot' deceived." There is a way which seemeth right unto a man, but the end thereof are the ways of death. (Proverbs 14:12 KJV) It's not right, but they don't want you to tell them that. I have been told; "Don't tell me that."

Much of that spiritual war is, many do not understand

what loving the world is, and/or what idol worship is. Anything that takes our time, love, and worship away from God, is worldliness, and if it "is an object", it is "an idol." God told Ezekiel 14:3-7 (KJV); "Son of man, these men have set up idols in their heart." We like to argue this concept; "What is an idol to one person, may not be to another", and many can't see, "made up 'spooks and goblins' as idols." There isn't anything about spooks, goblins, and/or any kind of witchcraft "that isn't idolatry before God" to start with. And any kind of entertaining it is idolatrous. And when we do love it, we don't love God, even though we claim we do. However, we must consider, "Ignorance" of the issue. However, sometimes; "ignorance is like a, 'bowl of delicious desert' and we can't see anything wrong with it, and we 'continue gobbling it down'."

When will we see, "God is not in us", when we are enjoying, being spooks, witches, goblins, and devils? When will we read and believe that scripture of, 1 John 2:15 (KJV)? On that Day of Judgment, Jesus won't know the professing saints and miracle workers who love and entertain the occult, for these are false practices, including "times of Old Testament Baal worship 'disguised'." God is not coming after a bunch of people working miracles in their communities, healing the sick, and doing wonders in his name, and many dressed up like witches; however, the scriptures tell us he is coming after a "glorious church, 'not having spot, or wrinkle'," (Eph. 5:27, KJV). Going through that strait gate and narrow way gets rid of spots and wrinkles, in our hearts and souls; however, Jesus did tell his disciples, "take care of the needs that are always present." (Mark 16:15-18 KJV)

And at the same time, we want those miracle worker around; however, Jesus told his disciples, they are the ones to do these miracles and wonders.

Again, if Christians love Jesus so much, why do they give Satan such a big Halloween party? And I am sure, real Christians don't. But what are "real Christians?" Think on that!

THE NATIVITY

Halloween isn't the only place our Christian community worships the Antichrist and/or Satan! (Revelations 13 KJV) The Nativity for years has been losing its meaning of redemption, "in our Christian Communities." We have, "Forgotten 'the reason for the season', but 'not in our minds', but 'in our hearts'!" Many who call themselves Christians no longer, "know the reason" --- "for the season", though they tell you they do, because they are, "deceived" and/or "very ignorant," but most likely both.

Back in the Old Testament, When King Ahaz was obstinate with the word of the Lord, Isaiah said to him; "Therefore the Lord himself shall give you a sign; Behold, a virgin shall conceive, and bear a son, and they shall call his name Immanuel," (Isaiah 7:1-17 KJV). In Luke 2:1–20 (KJV); "Shepherds found, "that virgin birth babe wrapped in swaddling clothes, and lying in a manger; because there was no room for them in the inn." In many of our "Christmas seasons", there is still no room for that, "virgin born babe" born in a manger, "to be 'in our hearts'." Our modern day Christian communities, "Christmas seasons" are filled with "the world 'celebrating holiday seasons'." Holy Days are a thing of the past in many, "so called Christians and their churches, and especially, 'in the Christmas season'."

Also in our "modern Christmases", we have city wide Christmas lighting, Christmas trees, yards and homes filled with Christmas declarations, flashing lights on a sleigh driven by Santa Claus, with reindeers pulling it, and our large department stores have large Christmas sells with children sitting on Santa Claus's lap, gifts everywhere, but no virgin born babe in a manger, and we are a Christian nation. Just who are we trying to kid? The Nativity "is there", but compared to the worlds declaration, just "barely there, and that is just in our mines." Our Christian community follows the world "in 'honor of the Nativity'," and the world doesn't honor the Nativity.

In the scriptures, this babe born in a manger, was given many names, titles, and identities and the following are some that we will mention in these memoirs, "Immanuel (God with us), Jesus, Christ, Son of God, son of man, Saviour, Redeemer, Lord, King, Alpha, Omega, begging, the end, and there are others." Concerning that, "First Christmas" the Shepherds couldn't keep it secret and spread the word around and went home glorifying and praising God.

In Matthew 2 (KJV), the wise men from the East came to the home where Jesus was, and when they saw the child, they rejoiced with exceeding great joy. Wise men still find Jesus and give to him, and worship him during the Christmas season, "because he becomes their savior", and will be the saviour to, "anyone else 'that believes' on his name."

However today, "deceived or worldly, 'so called' wise men" interact with Santa Claus during the Christmas season, knowing they are celebrating Jesus's birth, because deception is pure blindness, which only truth can heal. Again, we must know and want the truth before it can set us free (John 8:32, KJV). Compromising God's truth, and watering it down, "With 'Invented' things that become false doctrine, gimmicks, or 'Mythology'," sets no one free.

I see nothing wrong with dressing up a Nativity scene to honor Christ's birthday. However, our Christmas decor of today is so multinational, including every Nation and their special "holidays", and some nations don't even recognize the Nativity. But "many" in our Christian communities still call it celebrating the birthday of Jesus. Again, just who are we kidding?

July 4, 1776, our nation in the making had a good look at Jesus, and we got started off on the right foot, in spite of not being perfect. Through much praying and fighting, we went through Indian wars, and a Civil War, first and second World Wars, and God was with us, and was, "our help." However, after the Second World War, we let that Madilyn Murry remove some much needed praying in public places, that helped keep us close to God, and North Korea, Vietnam, and now, "The Middle East" gives us a lot of bothersome question marks. And recently again, "North Korea" is being a pain.

Down through the years, we turned our fashioning of things and holydays into tons of idolatry. Oh, how we have turned "the Nativity" into a gigantic conglomerate of beautiful things that can't be outdone, and so doing, we can't hardly see the Nativity, because it is so far in the back ground. The Christian community has taken this on, from our early USA beginning, and slowly let it grow into its massive Christmas glory, "without Jesus." The antichrist and all his false prophets have really pulled this off good, and we bought it. The Christmas season is everything except Jesus coming to this world as a babe to save sinners. The Nativity hardly gets honorable mention, even in many churches, and then just barely.

"We think" we know how the Grinch stole Christmas. I am still trying to figure out "what Christmas" the Grinch stole. Maybe it was the Grinch that stole the, "Reason 'for the' Season" from our hearts. We have lost the truth and reality of, "For God so loved the world 'that he gave his only begotten Son', that whosoever believeth in him should not perish, but have everlasting life," (John 3:16 KJV)

We could read John 3:16 like this; "For the 'god of this world' loved his god-ship so much, that he sent, his 'duplicates' of Jesus, riding in sleighs pulled by reindeer, and gifts to all that would believe on his name and honor him." Remember, Satan offered Jesus the world, if he would fall down and worship him. Jesus straighten Satan out on that issue/scheme. (Matthew 4:10 KJV)

However; Satan offered our Christian community Santa Clause loaded down with deceitful gifts, and we bought it. We have pushed the Nativity aside and down loaded Baal-worship from the Old Testament. Children setting on Santa's lap telling him what they want for Christmas, is a lot more fun and religious than singing, "Away in a manger."

Again, idols of the heart is anything that takes our attention away from honoring and worshipping our God Jehovah and his Son Jesus. (Ezekiel 14:3-4 KJV) If you take your children to the big department store to sit on Santa's Lap, and don't have time to go to the Christmas service on "said Sunday", you have and idol in your heart, "that may well", send you to hell. There is no place in the scriptures that tell us, "Christ will have a side kick to help celebrate his birthday." But our Christian communities sure have given him one, "and he is a 'fake', but multitudes loves that 'fake'."

We love "mythology", and we are building and writing and rewriting it all around God's truth. You can't beat the story, "It's a wonderful life", and some Christians think that story is so heavenly. Actually; "What 'is heavenly' about that story?" The many, "Christmas carols", which are a lot of "mythology making", are a large maneuver to direct our Christian community further and further from the Nativity, God's love, and God's truth. This is why Jesus said; "But in vain they do worship me, teaching for doctrines the commandments of men." (Matthew 15:9 KJV) Our worldly

Christmas mythology is not the doctrine of God, but of man, but oh how we love it.

You just try to get the Christian community to reject the conglomerate, for the Christian community know they are God's people and serving him, and will go to heaven when they die. However, a big part of our Christian community make their living by working in and for, "The Conglomerate," so we must keep the conglomerate, even though it is one massive tool of Satan. The Conglomerate is one of the main highways to the, "Antichrist and Mark of the Beast" (Revelations 13 KJV).

You talk about deception going to seed, springing up, and casting a cloud of beautiful things all over our Christian community, and our Christian community has no clue what is going on. You just mention it, and you will hear. "What are you talking about?" I know, because I have been there, and don't remember how many times. Again, John wrote, "Love not the world, neither the things that are in the world. If any man love the world, the love of the Father is not in him. For all that is in the world, the lust of the flesh, and the lust of the eyes, and the pride of life, is not of the Father, but is of the world. And the world passes away, and the lust thereof: but he that doeth the will of God abideth forever" (1 John 2:15–17, KJV). Loving our modern day USA's Christmas celebrations and festivities, "is loving the world, and a lot of it was put together by deceived people who call themselves Christians." Of course the world had their financial hands in it as well.

However, "If you have to have Santa Claus, Christmas trees, presences everywhere, and a house full of decoration and lights for you to have a very delightful Christmas, 'you don't have Jesus in your heart, and you are going to hell,' unless you repent and believe his gospel." That babe in a manger came to warn us of, "someone and/or somethings 'that would take his place', that are just 'many' phonies." People "who really 'know' Jesus" don't want Baal-Santa around their home anytime, for he is a false idol/god, which is the devil. I'll write this several times, "This babe in a manger came to warn us of, 'a bunch of phonies' coming to deceive us, and 'Baal-Santa' is one of the biggest." Everything that Saint Nichols of the third century evolved into, is nothing but, "idolatry and 'Baal-worship'."

However, our twenty first century, "Christian Christmas celebrations" are nothing but worldliness. However, "many would rather take their chance on, 'going to hell' than to repent and believe the gospel, of which that child, 'in a manger grew up and taught, repent and believe his gospel'." The tragedy here is, "According to Jesus, 'Many will'."

I have been invited to Christmas parties, where I was asked to bring a present to exchange that a man or woman could use. Those kind of parties have nothing to do with Christmas; however, it was in the Christmas season, with gifts given and received, so it was a Christmas gesture/function. "It was pure 'Christmas, Idolatry'." These kind of events are nothing but worldliness and idolatry, but many will continue, to show everyone, "we are in the 'Christmas spirit'." That whole concept is showing we love the world, and are enjoying our idolatry. We think Christmas is a great day for our Christian community, "and it must be 'celebrated'." When does all of that, "Worldliness and Idolatry" glorify Jesus coming to earth to save sinners, and to warn man there would be false prophets, false Christ, and false gospels, grace turned into Lascivious, and truth turned into a lie, that will do such? "We have 'accepted' what Jesus 'warned us not to accept'." Jesus said, "Be not deceived." (Luke 21:8 KJV) However, "many" are deceived, that know they are devout Christians.

Much of our Christian community, have thrown out Jesus and brought in, "Baal-worship." Baal worship includes and honors Satan himself, and the, "whole 'world' of worldliness."

The golden calf was a great day in the wilderness for the children of Israel, worshipping it. After all, "Arron, 'Moses' spokesperson" said; "These be thy gods, O Israel, which brought thee up out of the land of Egypt." That golden calf wasn't even made when God brought Israel out of Egypt. (Exodus 32:4 KJV) I don't remember how me times I have heard some Christian say; "Look what 'Santa' gave me for Christmas this year?"

Why didn't we ask, "Look what God gave me for Christmas?" At Christmas time, "Not Jesus, 'Not God'," but Santa is, "our god 'and gives to us'," That whole line, "Look what Santa gave me is phony," because Santa didn't give you anything, there was "another 'giver'." But you praised the, "Phony," and not the real giver. God is the "giver of life, 'giver of eternal life, and the giver of our life substance'?" When are we going to learn that? Oh yes, the world "will give us 'tribulations'," but Christ has overcome the world. (John 16:33 KJV) Why can't we give praise, "where praise is due?" But, being deceived, we will keep praising the phonies. Jesus did tell us; "The phonies will come and deceive many" (Matthew 24:5 - Matthew 24:11 - Mark 13:6 KJV).

Many who "halfheartedly believe in God/Jesus" become "very religious", and "idolaters," in our Christmas season, and some will make, "a very elegant dressed up church appearance," for the season. They are dressed up to be seen of man, not of Jesus. If you want to be seen of God, dress up your heart with, "God's 'Word'." Remember David wrote; "Thy word have I hid in mine heart, that I might not sin against thee" (Psalm 119:11 KJV). God's word in your heart, "is the best 'suit of clothes' you can ware anywhere, 'in this world'."

Many who profess Christ have no idea what the following scripture says. Jesus said, "For false Christs and false prophets shall rise, and shall shew signs and wonders, to seduce, if it were possible, even the elect" (Mark 13:22, KJV). It is hard for some to see these false Christ and false prophets are the works of the antichrist and his conglomerate, bringing all these worldly pleasures to deceive mankind and "professing Christians, and they are doing it, in 'Jesus name', and in and on 'Jesus birthday season'." You just try telling our Christian community today Santa and all his Christmas trees, decorations, presents, and great Christmas carols and/or stories has to go, for you to go to heaven, and see and hear their response; however, "these things will keep 'many' out of heaven?" But deceived people and fools don't see that.

Judge Jesus, on "His 'Day' of Judgment", which will be "Your Judgment Day" as well, will speak a lot of truth that people who claim to be his, will be traumatized after hearing him say, "I never knew you." You saying; "that isn't so", won't work here either. Again, at Christmas time, we can't see that babe in a manger, growing up, being crucified, raising from the dead, ascending into heaven, and is coming back for his own, "and being the 'judge of all that slighted', His Earthly Christmas Birthday Parties", to worship Santa, his Rain-deer, Sleigh, Christmas presents everywhere and under a Christmas tree, and a big Christmas dinner. *(Again, sorry about the long sentence, but let's leave it.)*

"But 'we don't worship' Santa Claus."

I keep hearing that; however, again, just who are we trying to kid? If Santa takes your time away from going to church and worshipping Jesus, "You are worshipping, 'Baal-Santa-Satan'." Read the Old and New Testament about Baal worship! It is all in there. The reason we don't know that is because, "we are 'ignorant'." The reason we are Bible ignorant is because we are no longer, "Bible students, or God's people." However, "we know we are Christians" going to heaven. We better put a lot of question marks right here, "???" for "there will be" a lot of people who call themselves Christians, going to hell.

35

"Thou shalt have no other Gods before me" (Exod. 20:3; Deut. 5:7; KJV). No man can serve two masters, for either he will hate the one and love the other; or else he will hold to the one and despise the other. Ye cannot serve God and mammon (Matt. 6:24, KJV). This scripture refers to one master as "money and/or greed." Is there another master in your life, other than God, "that you are trying to please?" Exodus 32 (KJV) tells us, the Children of Israel could not serve, "the golden calf and 'God both', but oh how they tried." 1 Kings 18 tells us Israel couldn't serve God and Baal both, but oh how they tried. First and second Kings tells us; Israel could not serve God and idols, "including idols of the heart," but oh, how they tried.

You can't love Santa, "which is 'a type' of the 'Old Testament' Baal-idol", and Jesus both and go to heaven. We have turned Saint Nickolas of the 3rd century into an evil figment of our imagination placed in our minds and hearts as an idol, and it replaces Jesus. About those other, "special interest things" we have hidden in our hearts. We must watch and not let our special aspirations become idols. God said to Ezekiel, "For every one of the house of Israel, or of the stranger that sojourneth in Israel, which separateth himself from me, and setteth up his idols in his heart, and putteth the stumbling block of his iniquity before his face, and cometh to a prophet to enquire of him concerning me; I the Lord will answer him by myself:" (Ezek. 14:7, KJV)

How are we going to convince Judge Jesus, Santa Claus and all his conglomerate isn't any kind of an idol we have in our heart? In the Christmas season, who gets most of our attention, "Lord Jesus" or "Baal-Santa?" Again, we must remember, "It's this 'Judge Jesus' is the one we 'slighted and snubbed' at 'His' earthly yearly birthday parties, so we could enjoy 'many or all' of the Worldly Christmas pleasures around, 'Baal-Santa'." What are the Christmas pleasures of this world? Here are "many, or at least some", of the facts; "Christmas trees, decorations, varieties of lights, poinsettias, presents, Santa Claus, his reindeer and sleigh," all of these had nothing to do with our Biblical Jesus or his birthday. We sure do love, "to replace the 'Biblical Jesus' with Baal-Santa and all his conglomerate."

How are we going to consider any of this, "Sins of ignorance?" We are going to have to have a real good lawyer on Judgment Day to get by that Judge. We probably won't even think about it, "but it was 'that babe' in a manger", that grew up and was crucified, rose from the dead, ascended to heaven, and was our "advocate/lawyer" in heaven, "but 'now' is our 'Judge', and it was 'his birthday party's' we shunned." And through all of this, "we claim," we know the reason for the season. No wonder Jesus said, when those false prophets show up; "Many would be deceived."

This child Jesus was worthy and had praise. Later, grown up and in his ministry, Jesus very well declared, "Verily I say unto you, inasmuch as ye have done it unto one of the least of these my brethren, ye have done it unto me" (Matt. 25:40, KJV). Jesus is worthy of our praise, but do we praise him? He is worthy of us ministering to him, but do we do it? He is worthy of us ministering to the needy, as giving into him, but do we? He is worthy of our faithfulness; however, does he have it, "Especially in the Christmas season?" (Rev. 17:14, KJV).

You can be sure Santa will get all the glory and praise he wants, and he is the phony. Why do we give phonies so much attention? According to Jesus; "Many would listen to the phonies, false, counterfeit, prophets, and be deceived." *(That's Just Plain Jim's version of the scripture, but it harmonizes with King James and the others. Matthew 24:11 KJV)*

A big Christmas party with "Baal-Santa", and him handing out presents, is a whole lot more fun, and "what's 'not' religious" about that? Our Christian communities have made Santa Claus, Christmas trees, and presents "a religious ritual and 'full of idolatry'." Many of our Christian communities, at Christmas time today, with all the Christmas décor, are so religious and at the same time without one trace of Jesus in their heart or mind, but it is a wonderful Christmas festivity, and we glorified Jesus. When does all of that really glorify Jesus, when your Idolatry took your attention away from the, "Nativity?" Baal-worship in Israel was nothing compared to our worship of Baal-Santa at Christmas time today. If you don't believe that, "you need to do 'a lot' of reading God's word and praying."

"OH, 'but we don't worship Santa'!" And quit calling

him "Baal-Santa," for he is just, "plain 'Santa Claus' to us." Calling him "Baal-Santa", offends us.

That plain, "Santa Claus" is a "plain phony" all the way.

"But we don't worship him."

I keep hearing that; how are you going to convince Judge Jesus of that, when he sees you in your, "Santa Claus Suite", handing out presents to your family, and you and your whole family were so busy, you didn't go to your Church Service, for the Christmas program? Again, remember it was this Judge Jesus, whose birthday parties you shunned, so you could spin time with Baal-Santa. Remember it was this Jesus that said; "No man can serve two masters." (Matthew 6:24 KJV) When you spend more time with Baal-Santa than with Redeemer-Jesus in the Christmas season, how are you going to prove to Jesus, you love him, but don't necessarily love Baal-Santa-Claus?

In Numbers 33:50-53 (KJV), God told the Israelites when they go into their land, they were to destroy all of the, "high places and idols of the inhabitants of the land." We don't see any need of that today, so we keep, "Our Baal-Santa."

The Day of Judgement will tell your story, whether you love and worship Jesus or Baal-Santa, and I hope and pray you will find Jesus before that day, if you haven't already?

Again, wise men still find Jesus, give him presents, and worship him. Again, the deceived wise men put on Santa Claus suits, hand out presents to their families, friends, and loved ones, not to the needy. However, "Absolutely 'no present with our Lord Jesus Christ's name' on it", and it was his birthday party. However, these wise men, "or goats in sheep skins", will ask; "When were we not 'givers' in the Christmas season?" *(My rewording of Matthew 25:31-46 KJV).*

How many whole churches, "pastors and all", are nothing but goats in sheep skin? (Matthew 25 KJV) According to Jesus, "Many." However, they will be surprised on the Day of Judgement, "that they are goats." Jesus said; "Many will say to me in that day, Lord, Lord, have we not prophesied in thy name, and in thy name have cast out devils, and in thy name done many wonderful works?" Verse 23 And then will I profess unto them, I never knew you: depart from me, ye that work iniquity, (Matthew 7:22-23 KJV- Also, Matthew 25:31-46 KJV).

Our "Christian Christmas Mythology with Santa Claus", tracks back to and from Saint Nicholas, of Patara, Turkey, and slowly became Saint Nick, Kris Kringle, and Father Christmas, and I have heard and read others, and all of these names we have let evolve into, "Santa Claus." When you take the "n" out of the middle of Sa"n"ta, and put it at the end of Sata "n" -- you have "Satan" himself. Spelling "S-a-n-t-a" is the deceitful way to spell Satan. No wonder Jesus said; "And 'many false prophets shall rise', and shall 'deceive many'." And boy have we been deceived. (Matthew 24:11 KJV) The Apostle John wrote; "Beloved, believe not every spirit, but try the spirits whether they are of God: because many false prophets are gone out into the world," (1 John 4:1 KJV). I have seen Christian's faces light up when Santa Claus was mentioned. Many don't get that thrilled when Jesus is mentioned. "But we don't worship Santa Claus!"

To many so called Christians, "The babe wrapped in swaddling clothes is 'old hat'." It is old hat to the deceived and lost, but not to, "God's Elect."

Why does our Christian community "mix in mythology" with the, "truth about Jesus" and on "his birthday?" Our Christmas mythology won't take anybody to heaven, but the grace and truth that came by our Lord Jesus Christ will. However, that "mythology" will take, "Many" to hell. Why do we make so much to do with, "the Mythology of 'todays' Christmases", and just "ignore the truth, and place it in the back ground as old hat?" Again, because "Many" who call themselves Christians, are deceived.

Saint Nicholas in the third century gave to the needy at Christ's birthday time, as well as other times. This has been used and known as a type of giving to Jesus at Christmastime. We must commend Saint Nicholas for him working miracles with the needy. When you give something to eat to one that is starving to death, you are working a miracle to that person and to God. The Salvation Army is about the only Judeo-Christian Saint Nicholas's we have left in that category today; however, I have seen some Santa Clauses around some of our Salvation Army workplaces. What are they doing there? They don't give to the needy! They give to each other. Well, they may show, "a little 'artificial' kindness" and brag about it now, and on Judgment Day! That could very well be their goal; however, Judge Jesus may not be impressed, because it was his birthday party they slighted.

We have learned this concept, "When we help the misfortunate at Christmastime, 'regardless of Jesus', 'we need Santa Claus'." Santa Claus has become that, "beautiful angel of light 'Jesus' in our Christmas season." Be careful how you reject that comment, because if you are a Bible student, you know it is true. We as Christians preach against "evolution" big time; however, "we practice it relentlessly 'in our idolatry'." Again, why do you think Jesus said; "Many will say to me in that day, Lord, Lord, have we not prophesied in thy name? And in thy name have cast out devils? And in thy name done many wonderful works?" (Matthew 7:22 KJV) But Judge Jesus will not be impressed.

Over the millenniums and centuries, we have evolved Saint Nicholas into one of the biggest antichrist of today. Santa Claus is one of the counterfeits of Christ being honored, "in 'place of Christ'." Jesus said, "I am come in my Father's name, and ye receive me not: if another shall come in his own name, him ye will receive" (John 5:43 KJV). And boy have we received him. Boy do we love and worship our Santa Claus. Better said; "Boy do we love, 'our polished-up Satan'." Again, remember, "Santa" is "Satan 'misspelled', but 'we still love him'." Oh God help us to wake up.

You do some real praying before you criticize that statement, because if you have any kind of a close relationship with Jesus, you know it is true, saying; "we don't really love and worship him." Again, just who are you kidding? You may not be worshipping Santa with your mouth, but your heart sure is, and that is where God is pondering, and listening. (Proverbs 21:2 KJV) There is nothing wrong with, "real Christians" singing often, "Search me oh God, and see if there be some wicked way in me?" In fact we need to sing that often, "as a prayer," and maybe every church service, and especially in the Christmas season?

You have wickedness in your heart, "if you slighted the Christmas service in your church 'to honor our Lord Jesus'," to make sure you had everything in order for your family's Christmas day with Baal-Santa. In the Old Testament, the prophets of Baal, "Rated Baal" to be the "Supreme 'god'." (1 Kings 18 KJV) Is Santa your supreme god? At Christmas time "he is 'a lot of people's' supreme god." Remember Satan, including Santa, is the god of this world, and to "many" that claim they love Jesus, "and know the reason for the season."

Again remember Jesus said; "They are worshipping me in vain." (Mark 7:7 KJV) In the days of the Kings, Israel was either serving God or the Devil. (1 Kings 18:28 KJV). Baal had a lot of different names. (Baal-Peor meaning, "lord of the opening," Deut. 4:3 KJV) (Baal-gad meaning, "lord of good fortune," Joshua 11:15-20 KJV) (Baal-hazor meaning, "Baal's village," 2 Sam 13:23 KJV) (Baal-hamon which means, "lord of wealth," Song 8:11 KJV) In Jesus day, "Beelzebub was the prince of the devils." (Matthew

12:24 KJV) And others. (This is my pen name on Santa, "Baal-Santa", and meaning, "phony giver.") But we love that phony giver anyway, and many will love him all the way to hell.

I read a cartoon a while back, about a little girl kneeling beside her bed, hands folded and praying, "Dear Santa Claus." Santa Claus has become a god/idol that infringes on Jesus, or takes his place completely that people worship every Christmas when it is Jesus's birthday. Santa Claus is nothing but an "evolutionary" product that Satan, "helped, 'God's People' to falsify" and invent from Saint Nicolas of the third century. That evolutionary product "is a phony", and only is real in our "mind and heart's 'deception'," and hasn't anything to do with Christmas or Jesus.

However, "many" people who call themselves Christians, "would rather 'worship and honor a phony' Santa," than a live Christ born in a manger, and they do. However, this phony Santa Claus, is a "Real-'Baal-Counterfeit' of Jesus." Again, this babe born in a manger came to warn us about these, "Many Phonies, 'that would come'," but we accept, "the phonies" with our arms wide open, but we don't accept the one that warned us of these phonies, especially on his birthday. Be careful how you judge that analyzes.

On the Day of Judgment there will be, "many" that know Jesus, that Judge Jesus doesn't know. And we could write it this way; On the Day of Judgement, there will be "many" that know "Santa", but "doesn't 'know Jesus'." Don't you dare think for a minute that isn't true? However, "are you one of them, 'that knows Santa' but doesn't know Jesus?" However, if you "know and love Santa very much" you don't know Jesus at all, even though you say you do, and say you love him. Jesus has no rivals at or in his birth or anyplace else, except in his death, he had two criminals crucified with him. (Matthew 27:38 KJV) And if we, "really love Jesus," we will be sinners and or criminals crucified with Jesus as well. (Galatians 2:20 KJV) Saints that are crucified with Christ don't keep religious phonies around, "Unless they are 'really ignorant', and or 'thoroughly deceived'."

Santa Claus is one of our biggest counterfeits of Jesus Christ today, but we will continue to use him in the place of Jesus, "though we deny it." We better remember God is so jealous he will not share his divinity with other want-to-be gods, regardless of who and what they are. If you have to have Santa, Christmas trees, presences everywhere around your house on Christmas, "and you 'still claiming you know the reason' for the season," don't count on Jesus knowing you on, "HIS" Judgment Day. The "very fact" that you have all of that Christmas junk/ stuff, is proof, "you don't know 'the reason' for the season." When you "really get 'to know Jesus', Baal-Santa has to go." Jesus will not have "any rivals" in your heart, on his birth day celebration, or on "His 'Final' Judgment Day", concerning you. He is the only one. You better, "deal with" this "ignorance now" that you have "with idolatry!" Idolatry is a "deadly 'sin', and its 'main road' is to hell."

Let me insert this right here, though we have mentioned

some of it. Often this idol worship slowly slips up on good Christians, and they have to deal with it. I have had that problem myself. Sometimes Good Christians has to "Clean House, because idolatry can really mess things up in your Christian life, 'if it's not clean out'." Been there, done that, and more than once.

Exodus 34:14 (KJV) tells us, "For thou shalt worship no other god: for the Lord, whose name is Jealous, is a jealous God." God help us if we love Santa Claus and his conglomerate. This Santa Claus network is large and worldwide. The big tragedy is, it is in people who claim to be God's people, that slowly helped it evolve over the millenniums and centuries, and it controls them. The Christian communities have been the biggest promoters of Santa Claus in our USA. Again, remember Jesus said, "Many false prophet shall arise and deceive, 'Many'," (Matthew 24:11 KJV). Santa Claus is a "Phony 'false' Christ", and is taking a lot of people who call themselves Christians to hell; however, how can you tell them that when they love Baal-Santa so much?" There are people who would rather go to hell than accept the truth, "of Jesus" and the tragedy is, "many will." You don't have to be one of them.

Here are some excerpts from scripture telling us what hell is. (Everlasting fire - Matthew 25:41 KJV) (Unquenchable fire - Mark 9:43 KJV) (Furnace of fire. There shall be wailing and gnashing of teeth. Matthew 13:36-42 KJV) (I am tormented in this flame. Luke 16:19-26 KJV) (These both were cast alive into a lake of fire burning with brimstone. Revelation 19:20 KJV) (Then shall he say also unto them on the left hand, Depart from me, ye cursed, into everlasting fire, prepared for the devil and his angels: Matthew 25:41 KJV) In flaming fire taking vengeance on them that know not God, and that obey not the gospel of our Lord Jesus Christ. (2 Thessalonians 1:8 KJV) (Here is the real bad notice; "Hell hath enlarged herself, and opened her mouth without measure: and their glory, and their multitude, and their pomp, and he that rejoices, shall descend into it." Isaiah 5:14 KJV) I would rather be crucified with Christ then go to that place. (Galatians 2:20)

But who believes in these scriptures now days? Our Christian community doesn't. We are in a "thorough deception mode", and don't see Jesus at all; however, we are claiming we know him. "However, 'in the Christmas season,' we still see a lot of, 'Baal'-Santa, and all of that, 'Christmas mythology', but not Jesus." Again, no wonder Jesus said; "Because strait is the gate, and narrow is the way, which leadeth unto life, and 'few there be that find it'." (Matthew 7:14 KJV)

No wonder Jesus did mention that there would be; "Many on Judgment Day boasting, 'of all they had done for him, and in his name'." However, Jesus said he would say; "I never knew you: depart from me, ye that work iniquity," (My paraphrase of Matthew 7:22-23 KJV).

"Oh, surely not? Jim that is just your imagination running away with you 'again'."

"You think so."

Well can you imagine what would happen, "if all Churches of God, and Christians would take a stand against Santa Claus, and all of its/his conglomerate?" It would cause, "the 'stock market' to have 'a large upheaval'." Much merchandise, "that fills the pockets of the Illuminati", would not be sold, and our Christian community would get the blame. However, it wouldn't be the fault of our Christian communities, "which are goats that claim to be in God's flock as sheep", because they would keep worshipping Baal-Santa, and buy and give gifts to all their friends and families. But it would be the fault of repentant believers, which are God's sheep that give to the needy at Christmas time as well as other times, as giving unto Jesus. However, "the repent Christians may not be many," to mess up the stock market, "in any way."

And this may be the time, "God would send his angels and, 'catch his Elect' away", and then the Christian community, along with the rest of the world, will see the, "unimaginable desolation." Read Matthew 24:22-31 (KJV).

Satan has seen to it that Baal-Santa has a sacred ritual in our Christmas season. I heard one time on the left wing media, that some atheist think Santa is a part of Christianity, and want him out of the way in the Christmas season, only they called it the, "holiday seasons." People who are Christians, "and those 'who call themselves Christians' are the blame for that." The thing that really gets me is; "Santa is a blessing to the left wing media," for he is one of their phonies that is glorified by them, with our Christian community, instead of glorifying Christ. Of course there are a lot of diversities in the left wing media to justify anything that is perverse or phony.

In general our Christian community doesn't see the Antichrist and the Mark of the Beast structure that is right in front of their eyes. Christmas and all its worldly glory is one of the biggest functions we have to push the Nativity out, and the Antichrist in.

Whether or not we care to talk about Saint Nicholas's giving, we must be aware, "we also need to give to the poor as giving to Jesus," not the giving to ourselves, our families, or one another. However, we are more inclined to love, "what Saint Nicholas has evolved into" and gives to our families and friends at Christmas time. We have abandoned the Christ of the Nativity but not our beloved, "Anti-'Christ' Baal-Santa." When we spend one Lord's Day a year in church service worshipping Christ on his birthday, and the past and present month, November and December, on Santa Claus, Christmas trees, decorations, and presents for the family instead of giving to the needy, who are we worshipping anyway? Maybe you better do some real praying before you even try to answer that question, and then do some repenting.

"Ah?"

"You 'just think', you don't need to."

Again, many times I have heard the words, thoughts, and excuses, "We don't 'really' worship Santa." He is just a, "beautiful lovable reminder, and function" of the Christmas season. "Anyway, our children have a good time with

Santa, the Christmas tree, and the presents. And, our children need to have all those 'precious memories'."

Let me remind you, "again" of what Jesus said; "Suffer little children, and forbid them not, to come unto me: for of such is the kingdom of heaven." What's wrong with taking Children to Jesus on "HIS" birthday, because Jesus would receive them? (Matthew 19:14 KJV) Jesus wouldn't promise them, "nicely wrapped junk/stuff" most of which they weren't going to get anyway. However, we would rather make our children, "the 'children of hell'," by taking them to the big department stores and let them sit on, "That Phony Baal-Santa's Lap" and tell him what they want for Christmas, which is the world's way of celebrating Christmas, because the love of the father, "and of Jesus" is not in people that do that. And people love the world's way of celebrating Christmas more than God's way. We could write it this way and it is truth. We love our "Baal-Santa" more than our, "Redeemer-Jesus." Don't you think for a moment; "Baal Santa isn't taking 'Many or Multitudes to Hell' every Christmas season, and 'at other times'."

"Oh, 'surely not' Santa 'can't be' that bad?"

You have forgotten, "Santa" is "Satan" misspelled. He may look lovable, "but he still is the 'real' Devil."

Anyway, what precious memories will our children have on the Day of Judgment when Jesus says to them, "I never knew you, depart from me, you worker of iniquity"? Be careful how you judge that comment, because a big part of our Christian community is sending their children to hell and most likely going there themselves. And you "not believing that, 'doesn't change' that."

This is a little bit spiteful; however, there "is an enormous amount of truth in it", Jesus could say; "Depart from me, ye cursed, into everlasting fire, prepared for the devil and his angels, 'you never came to my yearly birthday parties', cause' you are a bunch of old goats, dressed up like sheep, and couldn't get in." (My synoptic re-view of Matthew 25:41-45 KJV) Just remember, God is a jealous God, and doesn't share, "His, 'Divinity'."

"Oh, surely not that jealous?"

Remember, he is not only jealous, "He is also 'Holy', and 'Almighty'," and what he says stays.

Again, remember what Jesus said; "Not everyone that saith unto me, Lord, Lord, shall enter into the kingdom of heaven; but he that doeth the will of my Father which is in heaven." (Matthew 7:21 KJV) How is any of that Santa Claus, rain-deer, sleigh, Christmas trees, poinsettias, and decoration, "being 'the will of the father', when it is the world's way of celebrating Christmas?"

I have talked to other people as well; however, while back I mentioned Christmas to a, "Christian lady friend of mine." She broke out in smiles and told me, how her family really love the Christmas season, then she mentioned all the excitement, presents, Christmas trees, and of course "Santa", and especially the big Christmas dinner. She had everything in her Christmas festivities "plan" except Jesus, and she claims to be a Christian. I mentioned to her about Jesus birthday. She suddenly came back with firm convictions; "all of my family are well aware of 'the reason for the season'." My heart grieved for her family's souls, and I am praying for them.

Very few of our Christmas celebrations of today are, "Christ centered;" however they are, "thoroughly 'worldly centered', with the god of this world's blessings." Again, can you imagine how Satan is blessed with all of that? If you "really love Jesus" you won't "write off" what I just "wrote down."

We must remember this: our Christian communities of today have lost the reality of believing, "In the beginning was the Word, and the Word was with God, and the Word was God." They have also lost the reality of "The word was made flesh 'full of Grace and Truth'," born of a virgin, wrapped in swaddling clothes, and lay in a manger. But, they haven't forgotten how the Grinch, "and/or Baal-Santa" stole Christmas, "and 'the reason' for the season."

And, they haven't lost the reality of our beloved Santa Claus, his Christmas trees, his decorations, his presents, Christmas dinners, and all his Christmas pleasures and glory. Again, the "most clear and honest way" we can name Santa Claus is, "Baal-Santa," because that is, "exactly what he is." He is our "modern Old Testament version of 'Baal-god'." Don't you dare say, "That's not true." If you are any kind of a Bible student, and studied any Middle-east history, you know it's true. Again, Baal worship is not, "just a god/idol of the past." We don't seem to mind, "little 'satanic' things" reminding us of the Nativity/Jesus. Our feelings are, "Santa, 'can't be that bad'." And we can't see or understand, "Baal-Santa is taking a big part of our Christians community, 'to Hell'." (Matthew 25:41 KJV)

Don't you dare say; "Oh, surely not."

A little bit of poison want stop the sweetness of honey, "but it will still put you in the grave yard, 'six feet under'," after you have enjoyed it on toast with butter. Santa is "just that poison" to your soul. Remember, "Santa is Satan 'misspelled', but it doesn't change what he is."

In Acts 16 (KJV) we have the record of a demon possessed girl with a spirit of divination, which brought her masters much money. This demon possessed girl said about Paul and his men, "These men are the servants of the mosthigh God, that shew unto us the way of salvation." Paul was grieved that this demon-possessed girl telling everyone Paul is telling us about the way of God. However, Paul wrote to the Philippians, that some preach Christ just to grieve him, and he didn't particularly care for that; however, he was glad Christ was being preached (Phil. 1:15–18 KJV). However, this demon-possessed girl telling everyone Paul was preaching Jesus, "Really 'grieved' him."

The "message of the Nativity doesn't need any help from, 'Baal-Santa'," but the deceived will continue using him to be a blessing in their family Christmases.

Somehow we today just don't get grieved when Santa Claus, one of our antichrist or counterfeit Christs, reminding us of the real Christ and his birthday, who came to save us from our sins. Really, does Santa Claus remind us of Jesus? To many, I am afraid not, though they may say, "yes." We praise him for taking our attention away from giving to Christ, so we can give to each other, and we do a real good job of that. We don't want to believe this; "To 'many' of our Christian community, 'at Christmas time' are 'old goats', dressed up 'like sheep'." Again, a lot of our churches at Christmas time are full of, "Old Goats, dressed up like sheep."

Just how wicked are our Christian communities today, and especially in our Christmas season? Again, can you imagine how Satan is blessed when he gets all of that attention at Christmas time, "taken away from Christ, 'by the way we honor Santa Claus'?" This should be mentioned again; Satan couldn't get Jesus to fall down and worship him in the wilderness, (Matthew 4 KJV) however, he has well deceived our Christian community to worship his imitation Jesus, which is Baal-Santa, "or 'misspelled Satan'." Two thousand years ago, this Jesus warned us; "Many false prophets shall arise and deceived many." There isn't a bigger phony anywhere than "Santa Claus," and we love him so. Jesus reminders of the phonies that would come, "doesn't even bother us", because we love the world, and the world is full of phonies, which we "also love."

Again, our modern day Christmases fits perfect to Jesus' story of the sheep and the goats in (Matthew 25:31-46 KJV). The sheep give to the needy. The Goats took from Santa all the presents they could get, and gave to each other, but asked; "What needy brethren of yours have we over looked, and not helped." (My rewording.) Read the scriptures, and think about giving to Jesus, on his, "next 'birthday'!"

I know some that are reading these memoirs are saying, "Jim, you are getting a little beside yourself, 'again'."

You tell me that on the Day of Judgment, after Jesus tells you he doesn't know you. You better pray now that he doesn't say that to you then. I am not the sharpest knife in the kitchen; however, I keep my distance from the dull knife rack, by staying close to the knife sharpener, and his "words" are sharper than any two-edged sword. (Hebrews 4:12 KJV) And I have felt the sharpness of his "word" when he said, "Thou shalt have 'no other gods' before me," and you can't serve two masters at the same time. I also feel the sharpness in what Jesus said; "Many false prophets shall arise and, 'deceive many'." Are you one of, "that many?" Is his truth and or words, sharp enough to prick your heart with his, "words 'of truth', or is your heart just plain hard?"

I don't see anything wrong with a family having a big birthday party in their home to celebrate all the birthdays of the members of the family at one time. In fact, that would be real nice. I don't think it would hurt if someone would hand out the presents, even if he or she were wearing a monkey's suit of some kind. But what would happen if all members of the family got a present except one child? But "many" do that to the child of Bethlehem every year on his birthday. I wonder how much, "God is 'really' jealous" of his people doing that to his son. I know

I am still meddling. We should also read (Exodus 20:4-5 KJV) again, because "God does some 'real meddling Himself', in that scripture."

Really, I wouldn't mind if someone gave me a big birthday party, everybody came and everybody got presents, but it would be nice, if I got at least one present, being it was my birthday party. However, Jesus has to tolerate that every Christmas, by people that say they love him. Are we kidding, deceived, scripturally ignorant, or just plain "Bible stupid?" I know writing, "Bible stupid wasn't nice," but sometimes, "people who call themselves 'Christians are just that'," and sometimes they aren't very nice either. "Especially" when you disagree with them. Of course the words, "Unenlightened, uninformed, ignorant, or naive" would have been a little better way to write it. However, the words of Jesus are sharp and I would like using them to prick some hearts. His words are going to be more then sharp on the Day of Judgment, when he says too many, "Depart from me you workers of iniquity." Carbon/Diamond Razor Sharp, won't touch those words.

I think it would be nice for God's people that really love him would pray, "Jesus, you know what I have," and then asked, "What would you have me give to you this coming birthday of yours?" I doubt if Christ is asked that very much, and I haven't asked him that enough myself. But we don't mind taking our children to the big department stores and have them sit on Santa's lap and tell Santa what they want him to give them; "that they are most likely, 'not going to get' anyway." What can a phony give that's not in some form phony itself, and its parents that do the giving anyway?

I have never heard this question asked by a child sitting on Santa's lap; "Santa, what should I give 'to Jesus' on his birthday this year?" In general at Christmas time, people are not concerned about giving anything to Jesus. We give a few dollars to the Salvation Army and/or other groups, which do things for the unfortunate, and say to ourselves, "I gave something to Jesus." Did we really, or did we just pat ourselves on the back?

We don't want to believe this, however our idolatry has become so humongous and our way of worship, "is so protocol", we "can't see" anything in it, "that 'is not' scriptural." However, some of it is everything "but scriptural." The stable and manger had absolutely no added decoration, but they had Jesus. Today our churches protocol have piles of Christmas decorations, Christmas trees decorated, Poinsettias everywhere, and some things we just can't figure out, "what it is?"

"Many Churches" have everything in their church at Christmas time except Jesus, but we honored him with a good Christmas program. Most worldly churches worship Jesus, "this same way" every Christmas. I am also aware "some real Christians" worship Christ this way, "to their loss, 'because of ignorance'." Jesus said: "God is a Spirit: and they that worship him must worship him in spirit and in truth" (John 4:23-24 KJV). We should also worship Christ this way as well. Where is "The Spirit of God" in all of that worldly decoration and Santa Claus stuff? If you think the Holy Spirit is there, "you 'are' deceived, and ignorant."

We say we give to Christ on his birthday all of our praise and worship. Do we really? Where is our heart when we are giving him all of that, "lip service?" It's probably under the Christmas tree with all the presents. Sometimes our families are so excited about the Christmas tree, all the decorations, the presents, and our belly's so full of turkey, how would we ever have enough breath, time, and strength to sing "Away in a Manger?" That's not meddling, that's preaching, and some people don't know the difference, and sometimes "there isn't" any difference!

If we really love Jesus so much, why do we give Santa Claus, "such 'a big celebration bash' on 'Jesus birthday'?" Why not give, "Jesus 'that big bash'?"

Again, it is this babe in a manger that came to be, "Our Saviour", including, "our Judge" of all who "shunned his birthday parties", to give themselves a great big Christmas bash, with all the trimmings, according to our, "Modern Worldly Christmas Mythology" that we have accepted from our, "god of the world's, 'Baal-Santa's protocol'." And our Christian community loves it. I have wondered; "Could 'Satan spelled wrong', and pronounced 'Santa' be an addiction", that is lethal, or is it, "we 'love and want Santa' in spite of anything?"

It was this babe in a manger that came to be our saviour that would save us from hell, the lake of fire, the weeping and gnashing of teeth, and outer darkness. However, we have chosen to create a Baal-Santa, from Beelzebub of

Jesus day, including the Old Testament's Baal-worship, that would take us to the places that Jesus Christ came, "to 'save us' from." No wonder Jesus said; "Many false prophets shall rise, and shall deceive many." (Matthew 24:11 KJV) Are you one of the deceived? Serving God is no trivial matter. It's God and "Him only" we serve, and no relationships with any of the gods "of and in" this world, "that we want to drag alongside" with our Lord.

If you have Santa Claus in your, "Christmas Celebrations" you don't have Jesus, the one that came to save you from "the many Santa's, and other phonies," in your heart, unless you are, "really 'deceived and ignorant'." (Acts 17:23 KJV) (1 Timothy 1:13 KJV) There are people who are willingly ignorant. (2 Peter 3:5 KJV) Are you one of them? Paul wrote to Timothy; "Study to shew thyself approved unto God, a workman that needeth not to be ashamed, rightly dividing the word of truth." (2 Timothy 2:15 KJV)

"Many" in our Christian community do not want to believe this; however, "It is this, 'many' that are deceived" and going to hell; "But how do you preach that message, to our Christian community today?" It's hard to get that message preached behind our church pulpits today, when they are taken by false prophets, and/or "not caring Shepherds/pastors." Isaiah 56:11 (KJV) reads; "Yea, they are greedy dogs which can never have enough, and they are shepherds that cannot understand: they all look to their own way, every one for his gain, from his quarter."

EASTER

Here we go, "again" to another god and/or "idol" that we dearly love. Again, back in the Old Testament, we read how the children of Israel had a problem worshipping a golden calf and worshipping Baal, and these gods/ idols were made by human hands. Later God told Isaiah, "Israel is full of idols; they worship the work of their own hands, that which their own fingers have made." (Isaiah 2:8 KJV) However, we have beat Israel all to pieces on worshipping idols, and we do not see it because we are so biblically, spiritually dumbed down, and deceived, but most likely just plain backslidden. But don't you dare tell the Christian community that, unless you want to "bust a live 'religious hornet's nest' wide open." Our "lost Christian communities" doesn't want to hear the words, "You are going to hell, or 'depart from me you worker of iniquity'," because they are doing great works for God in Jesus name, and going to heaven. But Jesus, "will tell that 'to many' on 'His' Day of Judgment."

When it comes to loving, worshipping, and honoring

the resurrection of Christ, "some Christians" do a real good job of it. We have our early morning sunrise Easter service, which is good and people really show up. Then we have a well-planned Easter service in our church sanctuary. It is usually very good, and a lot of Christians that haven't been in, "Church since Christmas, 'are even there'." We have learned from the past, "they won't be back to church" till next Christmas, "unless there is a funeral, and 'the funeral could be their own'." And there are people "that only go to church, when they are 'carried in in a casket', and then some don't go to church then."

However, as soon as that Easter service is over, there is a commotion among all the children running to the side door of the church, to the yard where the, "Easter Bunny hid Easter Eggs" of all colors everywhere. I also noticed during the church service the children were not the only ones waiting, wanting, and "twitching" for that service to be over. That Easter egg hunt had so many preoccupied during the service. Who even remembers it was a service to celebrate the resurrection of our, 'Lord Jesus Christ'?" I know, I am meddling again, but it is about time God's ministers to start meddling against idol worship and false doctrine that has been put in place of God, which are sending souls to hell. Again, that is not meddling. "That 'writing' is 'preaching'."

Again, In Matthew 15:7-9 (KJV) Jesus said; "Ye hypocrites, well did Esaias prophesy of you, saying, this people draweth nigh unto me with their mouth, and honoureth me with their lips; but their heart is far from me.

But in vain they do worship me, teaching for doctrines the commandments of men."

The mythology that we have created, about the Easter bunny and his multicolored eggs "were" and "were not" considered pagan at first, however, some German immigrants earlier in the 1700s came and settled in Pennsylvania. Some date back as far as 1682 in USA, and earlier in many modern European Easter events, referring to an, "Easter 'Hare' bringing Easter eggs" of all colors for the children. Some of the first small rabbits were chocolate rabbits or bunnies, made to be "an Easter treat" if found by children. This mythology wasn't pagan to start with that we know of, but slowly crept into our Christian communities, and became an idol to take people's minds and hearts away from the resurrection of Jesus Christ. Of course at first, it was used to be a "child thing" to keep children busy and gave them something to look forward to on Easter. Satan is skilled in a lot of mythologies, and people, "including Christians", buy them, and especially when they are, "considered 'religious' episodes." Some people just love, "for other people to see them as 'very religious'." We need to get religion out of our hearts and Jesus into our hearts. Much, most, and maybe all, of our religion is nothing but "Idolatry."

And whether or not we believe it or like it, "That 'Mythology' is 'full of idols'." Again, (Isaiah 2:8 KJV) tells us; "Their land also is full of idols; they worship the work of their own hands, that which their own fingers have made." Why do we as Christians, "loving truth, loving Jesus, and loving his resurrection", have to create something that will become, "Mythology" to be practiced a long side with truth? Or could it be, we don't "really love truth 'as it is truth'?" So a little bit of making things with our own fingers, and loving that, can't be that "un-truth", so let's keep the mythology, 'that we have invented', that hasn't anything to do with, 'Christ Resurrection'." But, "we 'are not idol worshippers'!" Again, who are we trying to kid? You saying, "I do not have an idol" and you, "not having an idol" are two different things.

That "Easter 'Bunny and/or Hare' sends souls to hell, not heaven," but only the chosen and/or elect of God see that, and they are "very few." We invented that Easter bunny story and all his eggs out of our own minds and hearts, evolved from and with an age old pagan indulgences; "but don't you dare tell the people who claim to be the people of God that." Again, Isaiah saw, and then wrote; "Their land also is full of idols; they worship, 'the work of their own hands, that which their own fingers have made'." (Isa. 2:8 KJV).

Jim; "How can just a multicolored Easter egg be an idol?"

Read Isaiah 2:8 (KJV) again, and think about it. If that "Easter Mythology" wasn't used to take time and place from Christ's resurrection celebration, it most likely wouldn't be, "an idol, of any kind." You must remember also, it was created out of the world's traditions of celebrating Easter, and not God's word or doctrine, but oh how our Christian community loves that Easter Mythology more than the resurrection of Jesus.

Then again, look at the Easter Mythology in our Conglomerate making money filling the pocket books of the Illuminati and Antichrist? Just consider all of that "Easter clothing ware, Easter eggs, chocolate bunnies, and other Easter seasonal things sold in our retail stores? What does all of that have to do for the cause of Christ, and his resurrection? How much money from all of that, that goes into missions to win souls to our risen Christ?

But it was the Easter season, "and 'we celebrated' Easter."

That is right; "You 'did' celebrate 'Easter' but you 'didn't' celebrate the 'resurrection of Christ'."

That Easter bunny and all his eggs never had anything to do with the resurrection of Jesus, but boy it sure gets a lot of the attention, which we should give to our Lord's resurrection, on his, "said, 'resurrection day'," whatever day we call it. The golden calf and Baal didn't, and don't have anything on the Easter bunny and all his eggs, and/or Santa Claus, and our direct worship and honor of Satan on Halloween. However, here is the bad thing; we know that God, "will not hold these counterfeit Christs, idols, and all the other phonies against us" on, "His" Day of Judgment, when he says, "Depart from me, you workers of iniquity." Judgement Day is going to be a "catastrophic trauma" to a lot of people, "who know 'they are Christians'," and know they are going to heaven. If you do not believe that now, "on the Day of Judgment 'you will', but then, 'maybe' too late."

Just how vague can we get? God and his word has not changed. This is my re-wording of John 1:1 KJV, "In the beginning was the Word, and the Word was with God, and the Word was God, 'and still is God'." Do we have a zeal for God, but not according to God's knowledge, of his truth, or are we just plain Bible stupid? (Rom. 10:2 KJV) I know writing, "just plain Bible stupid isn't the nicest way to write it, however, there is a lot of truth there." We claim these are not idols or anything treasured as an idol. Again, just who are you kidding? The Day of Judgment will tell us who is kidding! You better make sure your salvation is worked out with fear and trembling before the Day of Judgment, or the Day of Judgment will give you a, "never ending trauma." The Apostle Paul wrote; "Wherefore, my beloved, as ye have always obeyed, not as in my presence only, but now much more in my absence, "work out your own salvation with 'fear and trembling'." (Phil. 2:12, KJV)

Again, "many 'knowing' they are serving, working for God, and doing all of this in fellowship with God are going to be traumatized on the Day of Judgment, because they are deceived, 'now'." (Matt. 7:23 KJV)

"Again, 'oh, surely not all of them'."

I don't see anything wrong with children having an egg hunt, because that can be a lot of fun, for real young children, especially if there is some small chocolate bunnies in it to eat. However, why do we have to make it to be "an 'Easter egg' hunt" and use it to take away "time and meaning" from the Easter resurrection story? I am also aware of the concept, "Easter is a pagan word and holiday." The resurrection of Christ happen during a "pagan occurrence" called Easter. Though Christians use the word Easter concerning the time of Christ's resurrection, they have no connections with pagan works. However, we have made, "Easter a 'pagan' occurrence."

I know some are legalistic about that and nitpick anyway, and some people think I nitpick, and I do. I nitpick we can only be saved by the grace of God; however, "to be saved by God's grace, we must first accept his grace", and "not frustrate it over, and over, and over with idols," but "many" will. (Galatians 2:21 KJV) We must grow in the grace of God, and not stay an infant in Christ. (2 Peter 3:18 KJV) We must "abound in 'this grace' also." (2 Corinthians 8:7 KJV) We must be taught by God's grace to deny ungodliness, and 'other gods and idols, and that includes Easter bunnies and eggs, and Santa Clauses', but "many" won't. (Titus 2:12 KJV) These "many" will have a "catastrophic trauma" on Judgment Day, and don't you dare think they won't.

CONCLUSION

"Again," God said to Ezekiel, "For every one of the house of Israel, or of the stranger that sojourned in Israel, which separates himself from me, and sets up, his idols in his heart, and puts the stumbling block of his iniquity before his face, and comes to a prophet to enquire of him concerning me; 'I the LORD will answer him by myself'" (Ezek. 14:7, KJV). Just "what all" did God tell us here?

God plainly declared, "Stop worshiping idols in 'your hearts'" (Ezek. 14:7 KJV). "For the eyes of the Lord run to and fro throughout the whole earth, to shew himself strong in the behalf of them "whose 'heart' is perfect toward him" (2 Chron. 16:9, KJV). A heart perfect before God does not have idols in it. I am the least in the kingdom of God, and I know it. However, my soul has been deeply vexed by our Christian community honoring Santa Claus at Christmastime instead of honoring Christ, and paying admiration to Satan at Halloween, instead of denouncing him, and giving attention to the Easter bunny that never existed, instead of uplifting the resurrection of our Christ that is coming back, to take us home. Let me ask a question this way; "Who 'in this group' that I have written about, is Jesus coming to take home?" Are you in that group?

Lo, this only have I found, that God hath made man upright; "but they have sought out 'many inventions'." (Ecclesiastes 7:29 - Psalm 106:39 KJV) Santa Claus and the Easter Bunny are "many" inventions, because there are zillions of them made, "that are pure phonies," that doesn't bring people to Jesus, but oh how we love them, when they are giving us such a fun time going to heaven, "not knowing 'we are really going' to hell." Remember Jesus said; "Many would be deceived." Are you one of them?

Why do people, "who claim they are God's people," with their own minds, hands, and fingers, invent something entertaining, enlarged it to take time and space, make it very pleasurable, and insert it in place of Christmas, Easter, and promote Halloween? We do this, "so we can 'evade the truth', and so doing 'evade the reasons for the seasons'."

On the Day of Judgment, that will cost us more than what we expect. Whether we see it or not, the Christian communities today are not the elect that God has chosen to be taken away from the great tribulations that is to come, and then the judgment. So "we will continue" to give Baal-Santa Claus his place of esteem, the Easter "Hare" Bunny and his fun time for kid's pleasures, and continue giving Satan what he wants on Halloween, and "we know" we are Christians going to heaven. When will our Christian community wake up, and know they are going to hell?

In the days of the Kings of Israel and the prophets, Israel never had to put up with Santa Claus, the Easter Bunny, and Halloween events, but "the gods/idols, and idols of the heart was a problem that separated them from God. Our community of Christians, "of today" don't seem to think; "Our present day idols and sins 'will keep us from God'."

Again, Jesus said; "Not everyone that saith unto me, Lord, Lord, shall enter into the kingdom of heaven; but he that doeth the will of my Father which is in heaven" (Matthew 7:21 KJV). Loving Santa Claus, the Easter bunny and his eggs, and worshipping Satan in his sanctuary, is first class, "Loving the world, and idol worship, and 'is not doing the will of our Father which is in heaven'." Again, the Apostle John wrote; "Love not the world, neither the things that are in the world. If any man love the world, the love of the Father is not in him" (1 John 2:15 KJV). But we will continue, "Calling God a liar", and tell people, "God is in us when he "is not." Calling "God a lair" is a serious transgression; however, often this is done in ignorance by being deceived. "Is God, 'still winking' at ignorance?" Read Acts 17:30 (KJV) again, answer that for yourself.

Why would Jesus say to these, "Come, ye blessed of my Father, inherit the kingdom prepared for you from the foundation of the world" (Matt. 25:34, KJV)? Be careful how you judge that point and question. Again, remember he is coming after a church without spot or wrinkle, and loving Santa Claus, the Easter bunny and his eggs, and glorifying Satan on Halloween is a lot of wrinkles, and "God's 'Elect' does not have these wrinkles, For they are the Called, Chosen, and Faithful" (Rev. 17:14, KJV). Are you one of them?

Let me ask this question; "Are you a Christian going to hell?" Again, claiming to be a Christian and being a Christian are two different things. Which are you? Here is the big question; "Is our Lord really coming back after the people I just wrote about, 'or his chosen'?" We must again remember; "Many are called 'but few' are 'chosen'." (Matthew 22:14) Which group are you in, the "many" or "the few?"

That Great Judgment Day will tell us a lot of stories, and many of the responses to those stories will be, "I never knew you, depart from me you worker of iniquity" (Matt. 7:23, KJV). We better read and do what the Apostle Paul wrote to the Corinthians: "Examine yourselves, whether ye be in the faith; prove your own selves. Know ye not your own selves, how that Jesus Christ is in you, 'except ye be reprobates'?" (2 Cor. 13:5, KJV)

Again, Paul wrote to the Philippians, "Work out your own salvation 'with fear and trembling'" (Phil. 2:12, KJV). This scripture tells us we better be dead serious about believing down deep in our hearts that Jesus Christ is our Lord, without any attachments to other gods, in and of this world. God's eyes are searching for hearts that are perfect toward him, without being attached to other fantasies that we idolize (2 Chron. 16:9, KJV). This calling to serve God is eternal life to the chosen. The chosen only serve one God, and they don't pay tribute to other, "wannabe 'gods' along the way."

How many gods do you have in your closet, or your heart, and in your activities that you address regularly? Titus 2:14 (KJV) tells us Christ gave himself for us, that he might redeem us from "all iniquity," *(whether or not we want to believe it, that includes idols, and idols of the heart.)* and purify unto himself a peculiar people, zealous of good works. Peter wrote, "But ye are a chosen generation, a royal priesthood, a holy nation, a peculiar people; that ye should shew forth the praises of him who hath called you out of darkness into his marvelous light" (1 Pet. 2:9, KJV).

Let me paraphrase this scripture, Peter wrote; "But ye are a chosen generation, a royal priesthood, a holy nation, a peculiar people; that you should shew forth the praises of him who hath called you out of darkness, "which 'was and is' a humongous multitude of idolatry", into his marvelous light. Idolatry "is not" a thing or sin of the past. Today, it is very dominant in many of our churches.

There are Christians that turn their back on Santa Claus and all his Christmas trees and presents, the occult and all of the Halloween fun, the Easter bunny and his eggs, and the idols that could be in their hearts. These are a very peculiar people, and compared to our Christian community, "they also are 'very few', and 'the only ones going to heaven';" However, the world doesn't seem to care for these kind of Christians. (John 15:18-19 KJV)

Also, our Christian community doesn't seem to care for them either.

Years ago, I denounced the occult, Santa Claus, the Easter bunny, and a lot of other things God has dwelt with me about to only serve; "The word made flesh, full of grace and truth," and I don't mind being a peculiar person. I am re-denouncing these counterfeit Christs, false prophets, false concepts, and their false doctrines, for the truth that is in Christ Jesus my Lord, who died in my stead on Calvary.

Our Christian community churches will continue worshipping these other gods and antichrists until they are washed in the blood of Jesus and born again of his Spirit. Again Jesus said, "Strait is the gate, and narrow is the way, which leadeth unto life, and 'few' there be that find it" (Matt. 7:14, KJV). The occult, Santa Claus, and the Easter bunny, and idols of the heart won't help you find that "strait gate." In fact, they will lead you far away from it, but make you believe they are taking you to it, and through it.

Again, why do God's people love things that are as phony as the Easter bunny and Santa Claus? What is wrong with loving "A living Jesus" at Christmas time, and loving and "celebrating Jesus resurrection" at Easter time? At least Jesus is "still alive, well, and is on constant duty as our advocate/lawyer in heaven." (Hebrews 2:17 KJV) (Hebrews 3:1 KJV) (Hebrews 4:14-15 KJV) The truth is, "they are deceived."

During the Halloween season, the world needs Jesus,

but our Christian community gives the world spooks, witches, devils, goblins, and ghost. "But we don't worship and honor Satan." Again, just who are you trying to kid. God knows where your heart is, and what is in it, and knows what your heart loves, and worships.

During the Christmas season, what the world need is Jesus; however, we give the world, "a lot of 'phonies' such as Santa Clauses, Reindeers, Sleighs, and Christmas Trees with all of its splendor decorations, but 'we don't worship Santa'!" However, many were so busy, they didn't have time to sing, "Away in a Manger," and "many" probably have forgotten the words to it anyway.

During the Easter Season, we need to present to the world, "A Risen Savior", but we give the world, "The works of our own hands and fingers, in many different colors, 'but they are not idols'. Just who are you/we, still trying to kid?"

Over the centuries and millenniums we have put together volumes of books on mythology, about every form of man's history. We as "so called" Christians have written and rewritten, our mythologies, and "believe it as, 'Christian mythology', and 'Easter mythology'," however, there is no Christianity in it. "It is full of 'the devil'." God's truth does not need contaminated with Satan's "Baal-Mythology," but many will continue preaching and teaching, "the commandments of men" for "the doctrines of God."(Matthew 15:9 KJV)

Again, Jesus told his disciples, "be not deceive". He also told them, many would be deceived. Many false prophets would come and deceive many. The real bad thing here is, "The world loves phonies," and when Christians are like the world, "Christians love phonies." The Easter bunny and Santa are phonies, and our Christian community loves them, and will love them all the way to hell.

If we are ignorant of these phonies, and we repent and believe Christ's gospel, Christ will save us. If you are holding on to, "loveable phonies" remember, they won't get you into heaven, but they will take you to hell. All phonies are works of Satan. There is nothing phony about Jehovah God, His Son Jesus, and the Holy Spirit. Our God is a God of nothing, "But Truth and Holiness" and he shall remain that. God said; "For I am the Lord, I change not; therefore ye sons of Jacob are not consumed" (Malachi 3:6 KJV).

Christ and his gospels warned us of these phonies, but if we don't have any spiritual understanding, we won't understand it then. Some people refuse spiritual understanding. Jesus said, this is why I speak to them in parables: "Though seeing, they do not see; though hearing, they do not hear or understand. When anyone hears the message about the kingdom and does not understand it, the evil one comes and snatches away what was sown in their heart. This is the seed sown along the path. But he that received seed into the good ground is he that hears the word, and understands it; which also bears fruit, and bringeth forth, some an hundredfold, some sixty, some thirty." (Parts of Matthew 13:13-23 KJV) How many will disregard these memoirs, "as nothing to be concerned about" and go to hell?

Thanks for reading my observations, memoirs, opinions, "meddling's", and sermonettes. — Jim Howard

Ps., remember this; "Believe on the Lord Jesus Christ with all you heart, mind, and soul, and that he was crucified on the cross, was buried, rose again, went to heaven, and is coming back after his Elect, and you will be saved." Parts of (Romans 10:9-10 KJV) (Acts 16:31 KJV), and other scriptures.